CW01666974

Beir Bua

Press

www.BeirBuaPress.com

Thrills and Difficulties: Being a Marxist Poet in 21st Century Ireland

by

Kevin Higgins

Published by Beir Bua Press

ISBN: 978-1-914972-07-2

Beir Bua Press, Co. Tipperary, Ireland.

Typesetting / Layout, Cover design: Michelle Moloney King

Cover image - Taken by John Cunningham

Ordering Information: For details, see www.BeirBuaPress.com

Published by Beir Bua Press

Printed in the UK

9 781914 972072

for Susan who listened to all this

Thrills and Difficulties: Being a Marxist Poet in 21st Century Ireland

Kevin Higgins

Author's Introduction:

This essay was my project for the ghastly first months of 2021. Unlike most of what I write, it was not written in one sprint but piecemeal, three or four hundred words at a time. Usually when it was dark outside. During the lockdowns I found time to read a huge amount of literary theory. This essay is in part my small attempt to add to Marxist literary theory by using my no doubt idiosyncratic understanding of it to give recent developments in Irish poetry a fairly robust autopsy. What does it mean to be a Marxist poet? It has nothing to with wanting to impose communism on the known world, though that sort of thing can be fun. What it really means is being someone who both interprets the world poetically and knows that if you don't understand what capitalism is doing to humanity, and this planet we for now call ours, then you don't really understand very much at all. It also means being prepared most of the time to be in a small minority in the literary world which, particularly in its power wielding upper echelons, is dominated by liberals who broadly sympathise with the Barack Obama / Katherine Zappone / Kathy Sheridan of The Irish Times wing of things as they are. To paraphrase Travis Bickle: I don't hate these people, I just think they are silly. And that this silliness could, if the cards fall the wrong way over the next few years, lead us towards a Postmodern version of the disaster that was the1930s and early 1940s. The essay is written in the polemical style I favour. It will annoy many. And I will view their annoyance as a compliment. It is also personal. Ultimately, it is the story of how I didn't end up like William Wordsworth, though of course I haven't ended yet. Wordsworth was a young enthusiast for the French Revolution – "Bliss was it in that dawn to be alive" – who in later years became a fossilised reactionary, even writing a pretty awful poem, 'Protest against the Ballot', in which old Willie declaimed his opposition to the Chartists and their crazy notion of giving working class men the vote. There has been much such turning of the coat by literary gentlemen down the past couple of centuries. Saul Bellow, Samuel Taylor Coleridge, Conor Cruise O'Brien, John Doss Passos, Max Eastman, Robert Southey, and John Osborne – to name just a clutch – all started out as radicals of one stripe or another and ending up as shricking right wingers who, did things like vote for Nixon/Thatcher/Reagan, or support the use of torture by the Gardaí against Republican suspects in the 1970s. During the few years (about 2006-2013) during which I tried to believe that our existing political world set up might be preferable to any alternative, I never went as far as that. But by 2010, it's fair to say I was in some danger of becoming a sort of Neoconservative. It got so bad that one of my poems was even praised by Tony Blair's fan-boy biographer John Rentoul in the London Independent, another by Iraq War enthusiast, the former journalist Nick Cohen, who described my 'The Eternal Peace Activist' as "a poem for our times". They were dark and terrible times. But a necessary learning curve for me, which I embarked on for what I still think were understandable reasons. So, yes, in many ways this essay is above all memoir. A much compressed version of the story of a poet who appeared to be abandoning his youthful Trotskyism for literary liberalism of the Cruise missile variety, but who was talked out of that apostasy by the sheer silliness and venality of your average common or Town Hall Theatre literary liberal.

Kevin Higgins, 3/8/2021

Thrills & Difficulties: Being a Marxist Poet in 21st Century Ireland

for Susan Millar DuMars

More than a quarter of a century ago a man-child called Kevin retired from politics as he turned twenty seven. He had joined the then somewhat notorious Trotskyist group, the Militant Tendency[1], at the age of fifteen. After twelve years of activism, which began as a member of Galway West Labour Youth the month the Falklands War kicked off and fizzled like the saddest of fireworks in London in the aftermath of Mrs Thatcher's Poll Tax, against which he had been a somewhat obsessively focussed campaigner, it was over. "Retirement" was the face-saving word he used to describe his departure from politics. From the inside it felt like a personal tragedy. And it was. After more than a decade as a fiercely loyal 'comrade', Kevin had had enough of Militant and they had had enough of him. Dialectics being the contradictory beast it is, a total exit from active politics may have been the best thing that could possibly have happened to him right then. But it didn't feel like that to him. Instead of world socialist revolution, with which history had refused to oblige him, the spectres haunting the little part of Europe with which Kevin was then mostly concerned were, from his point of view, disappointing: Tony Blair and the Celtic Tiger, which got given its name the same year Blair became UK Labour leader: 1994.

---

[1] Trotskyist organisation which worked inside the Irish & UK Labour Parties, particularly during 1970s & 80s

Kevin sloped back to Galway from London via the Holyhead ferry that April with a mouthful of bad teeth; he wasn't much of a one for looking after himself then. Though would march to defend the NHS for other people until his shoes disintegrated; he did not partake of such services himself. Kevin arrived in Galway with no particular plans, apart from a notion that he might do something artistic. Not artistic in the prettifying sense; he had no interest in describing the rocks around Connemara and the like. Indeed, he had little interest in any kind of beauty. Or so he thought. He wanted to express things he had been unable to say during his years as a (partly self-appointed) leader of the vanguard of the North London semi-lumpen proletariat. Mostly, this would involve going into some detail about all the people and ideas and institutions he was against. It was no small list. High on it was his endlessly self-sacrificing former self, who had worked himself some of the way towards a possible early grave, in an attempt to fight the political tide of the early 1990s that was, in the end, more about masochism than socialism. By "doing something artistic", he meant stuff to do with words – songs, poems, maybe plays, novels... In the last years of his activism, when he was Chair of Enfield Against The Poll Tax in the North London Borough then represented in the House of Commons by, among others, Michael Portillo[2], he had become increasingly focussed on how best to say what needed to be said. It wasn't enough to say it. It had to be

---

[2] Member of Margaret Thatcher's later governments

said well. And, if possible, said wittily. He didn't know it at the time but writing political letters with a satirical bent to the local papers in Enfield in the very early 1990s was his beginning as a poet.

This Kevin, who was of course me, hoped to escape politics via poetry but also harboured illusions that he might somehow find a way of combining the two. It is a contradiction I have been working out ever since. From the inside it has felt more to be a case of this obvious contradiction working itself out using me as a somewhat extreme public example. Of late this contradiction has grown starker and as a result perhaps been somewhat resolved. In the course of my work as a poet, I regularly meet that strange creature, the literary liberal, who ascribes to themselves every progressive and humane value while at the same time apparently finding no place in their imaginations for even the possibility of a world not run in the interests of Jeff Bezos, Elon Musk, and Apple Inc. They are the sort of people who, if they didn't necessarily agree with her, would at least have understood where artist Tracy Emin was coming from when she called David Cameron's coalition of 2010-15 "the best government...that we've ever had". Politically, Emin may be an ignoramus. But her incontinent mouth is useful in that it makes her spell out what others in the arts are only brave enough to occasionally think. It has been my experience that, post 2008, most established literary creatives cannot imagine as possible a world in which a substantial percentage of the populations of countries such as Ireland, Britain, and the United States don't live in Victorian levels of poverty. Just look at the queues of homeless being fed each Friday night outside the GPO in Dublin by the charity Muslim Sisters of Éire. Despite such images, the idea of properly taxing the super-wealthy, and making sure they don't find a way of avoiding that tax, is seen by your average sensible member of the literary classes as a notion only seriously held by annoying teenagers and people who think it's still 1975. According to this broad school of thought, if it can be called thought, there never was any other possible solution to 2008 but spending less on the lower orders and using that money to bail out JP Morgan, Anglo-Irish, and the Royal Bank of Scotland in the hope that the pre-slump status quo could somehow be restored. So your average literary stuffed jacket, or pants-suit, tends to quietly cut characters such as Varadkar, Obama, and Cameron a huge amount of slack. As long as they give them things like a side of same-sex marriage to go with all those hungry schoolchildren and people sleeping in wet cardboard boxes. The same lit-libs who, should your criticism of things as they now are become too harsh, will leap to list off the (actually very short) list of good things people like 'Barack' and 'Leo' did while leading their respective countries, and then pull the sort of face one does while having a catheter inserted if you dare suggest some bit of communist craziness such as that, to pay for the Covid crisis, Ireland should consider increasing its notoriously low corporation tax rate from the current 12.5% to, say, 13% for the next five years. An increase of just 0.5%. Once the pain of the metaphorical catheter insertion passes from their hugely tolerant face, it will be replaced by the faraway, superior look of a 1980s Irish religion teacher trying to move past the appalling fact that one of their students just said the word "abortion". Then they will look at you and say something like: "but you've always thought that, haven't you." It's a variant of Mandy Rice-Davies'[3] "He would say that, wouldn't he."

They offered similar responses if they thought one was getting irresponsibly enthusiastic about the movements around Corbyn and Bernie Sanders, or Syriza in Greece in 2015, or the successful anti-water privatisation movement in Ireland or, if they are that particular sort of American, the idea of Medicare for all or a minimum wage of $15 per hour. It's a way of reducing what the person to their left is saying to a collection of perceived dogmas they no doubt think one has held to fanatically, like some dusty bedsit socialist ten commandments, since Arthur Scargill[4] were a lad.

Nothing could be further from the truth. Marxism is something I spent several years actively trying to get away from. But couldn't. Precisely because the ideas that dominate the mostly middle class poetry world, in which I have been immersed for two decades, are so absurd in comparison. It is precisely because of this lack of intellectual seriousness, which looks increasingly obscene set against events; not to mention its by product: the

---

[3] Welsh-born model best known for her her role in the Profumo affair, which discredited the Conservative government of British Prime Minister Harold Macmillan in 1963

[4] President of the UK National Union of Mineworkers during their 1984-5 strike

almost comical chancerism and opportunism which literary liberals call "networking", that has led me to start acting and thinking in an overtly Marxist way again, since around or about 2014. The networking phenomenon lately reached possible apotheosis with one of Ireland's premier literary resource organisations using its website to advise beginner writers to get a professional headshot taken and some business cards made. It went on to suggest new writers take a course with said organisation which would, among other things, help them in building their "brand" as a writer. Marx predicted capitalism would, in time, magic everything into a commodity. And now an Irish state funded arts organisation proves him right by overtly urging young writers to see themselves as commodities from the start. I am though a different kind of Marxist to the one I was thirty years ago, far less party orientated, far more concerned with the broader movement. I again have people all around the world who I consider comrades. People who, though their faults may be many, try to resist the current fashion for putting oneself up for sale at what usually turns out to be a pretty low price.

From about 2006 to at least 2012 I was what can best be described as a collapsed Marxist. Not collapsed (and also a little bit Marxist) in the sense that Brendan Behan sometimes was due to the presence of too little blood in his Champagne. Rather, still Marxist in the way I viewed the world but collapsed in the sense I could see no way of applying it to the stuff happening around and about me. Socialism, what little remained of it, appeared to have fallen in love with its own marginality. A good minority of those who remained on the socialist left on the eve of the global financial coronary of 2008 seemed to me to be oddballs and cranks who had nowhere better to be; or, at the very least, to have developed an excessive tolerance for such refugees from reality. This perception was hardened greatly by the fact that a couple of stage four literary cranks with leftist pretensions happened to operate right here in Galway. And the pre-2008 Left locally was only delighted to opportunistically clutch said oddballs to its haggard bosom.

Every time the Arts Council declined to fund some bit of pseudo-literary crankery - the sort of events to which no one turns up and then someone runs screaming out the door - the Left lined up to sign petitions and letters protesting this outrage. It was one of those classic romances between two lonelies, driven primarily by the fact that almost no else wanted to know either of them by that point. I know my reaction to it was excessive. It led me for a period to dismiss everything the Left, which at bottom was still my tribe, had to say. Hugo Chavez and Eva Morales[5] clearly weren't to blame for weird letters every other week in the Connacht Tribune from minor poets with issues. Yet, in my mind, the two became conflated. My reaction did spring from material reality. I felt let down by the obvious stupidity of what was supposed to be, broadly speaking, my own side. Why should I believe a word they said about Venezuela or Bolivia or Iraq when they talked what I knew

---

[5] Left wing President of Bolivia 2006-2019

to be raw horseshit every other month in the local media, and online, about funding for the arts in Galway?

It wasn't just little local neuroses that made Marxism seem inapplicable in the pre-2008 world of up, up and away capitalism. As Terry Eagleton wrote in his introduction to *Marxist Literary Theory* in 1997: "Marxism, then [after the collapse of the Soviet Union in 1991] was taken to be less disproved than discredited, out of the question rather than out of arguments." This was the intellectual atmosphere in which, by then, twenty eight year old me, who'd spent 40% of his life as an active Marxist, began writing poetry. My first two poetry collections *The Boy With No Face* (2005) and *Time Gentleman, Please* (2008), which established me as a poet, whatever 'established' exactly means in this context, were both entirely written between 1996 and 2007, years when the neo-liberal strain of the capitalist virus was the only ideological infection in town. To such an extent that one hardly ever heard anyone saying the c word. Capitalism wasn't a system particular to a time and place, in which we just happened to be living. Rather, it was just how things are, and how they would always be, like the Divine Right of Kings in seventeenth century France. Only more so. For in the mid seventeenth century Louis XIV[6] for a time faced a formidable challenge across the Channel in the form of the republican government in England, in which the poet radical John Milton was an advisor and was commissioned by Oliver Cromwell to write *Defensio Secunda*, a pamphlet

---

[6] King of France 1638-1715. Also known as the Sun King.

in defence of Parliamentary government. When I started writing poetry, even to say the word 'capitalism', or to write poetry which acknowledged said system's existence marked one out as some sort of ex-Marxist peculiarity because if you knew the word capitalism you could only have been taught it by socialists. One felt like an alien. I remember attending an open-mic poetry reading at the Apostasy Cafe in Galway in 1998 and talking to an alluring young lady with a gold standard south of England accent. She informed me, without blinking once, that she and the then recently late Princes Diana shared the same astrological sign and that, as a result, she had a profound and personal connection with the late Princess's soul. I said nothing. But looked at her and then around the room at the assembling crowd and knew that my ideas about the world would, to most people there, have seemed far more eccentric than hers.

These days, I often have a similar feeling of being a strange life form who has somehow landed in the Irish poetry world from another dimension. But I view the fact that I am now semi-detached, some days almost entirely detached, from Irish poetry, while also being in a sense part of its establishment, via the readings I co-organise, the reviews I write, and the workshops I run, as a radical success, and an outcome my much younger self would have enthusiastically endorsed. About eight years ago I began publishing more and more poems, especially contentious political poems, online, usually on political and news websites and blogs, places in which poetry is unusual. I couldn't see the point waiting weeks or, more usually, months, for a journal editor to get back to me when the poem seemed to demand that it get out into the world more urgently than that. Plus, the internet now offered the possibility of thousands of readers for a poem, particularly through building a connection with people interested in political action as well as talk. In 2013, five years before the 8th Amendment was repealed here, I published my then new poem 'Irish Government Minister Unveils Monument to Victims of Pro-Life Amendment' on the website of Dublin Fingal TD, Clare Daly[7], who has been a friend of mine since our time together in Militant. I wrote the poem shortly after the death of Savita Halappanavar who died after being refused an abortion in our local hospital, which you can see from our kitchen window. The poem has been re-published many times and in 2014 I was passing a small boarded up building at the very bottom of Quay Street in Galway and noticed that someone had, without my knowledge, made a poster of the poem and pasted it onto one of the boarded up windows. The fact that whoever it was went to the trouble of printing the poem out and pasting it there clearly meant that it spoke to them, independently of the gatekeepers who like to think they decide what poetry is. I was happy to bring poetry into the heat of what was then a contentious political battle. I could have sent this poem, which later appeared in my collection *The Ghost In The Lobby,* to Poetry Ireland Review or some other top magazine. But what would have been the point? I know that there are many poets who take the

[7] Member of Irish parliament (Dáil) 2011-2019 & European Parliament since 2019

opposite view and think it better to be read by less people, if said people are of a 'better quality'.

Walter Benjamin wrote of the Surrealists, who began as a movement of poets, that they sought to construct a literature where "the 'best' room is missing". My grandmother's house had a best room which always seemed cold because a fire was hardly ever lit in there. It was where her dusty fine China cups resided. When she had the Stations Mass in the house every few years, as was the custom at the time, the priest and the men were always served breakfast afterwards in that best room. These days when I pick up quality literary journals, or read the programmes of literary festivals that consider themselves 'elite', I think of my grandmother's version of Walter Benjamin's best room and update it to have some poet, who everyone else in that chilly little room agrees is marvellous – for that is the price of admission – taking the place of the priest. If the choice is to either have one's poems pasted illegally on boarded up buildings or to be well thought of by those who inhabit that room, I'll choose the former. Though, such binary choices aside, if you run a literary festival, or top magazine, and wish to invite me to dine, I will likely accept and my table manners will be impeccable. I will eat everything you put before me.

Increasingly, though, what first strikes me when I read contemporary poetry is not that it is either particularly good or particularly bad but that it mostly doesn't matter. It is of course hugely important to the participants in the poetry networking game in the way that the Best Kept Garden competition is of great import to those residents of Midsomer[8] who participate. Much contemporary poetry seems to me to be paralysed by an absurd respect for existing institutions and, in particular, the sacred institution of private property. This didn't matter much in the pre-crisis years, when history was supposed to over and socialism in the cemetery. But it matters now. Most of a century ago, the French poet Paul Eluard, who was first a leading Surrealist then a committed Communist, wrote the following, the translation is by David Gascoyne:

Critique of Poetry

Of course I hate the reign of the bourgeois
The reign of cops and priests
But I hate still more the man who does not hate it
As I do
With all his might

I spit in the face of that despicable man
Who does not of all my poems prefer this *Critique of Poetry.*

It is impossible to imagine any member of the self-selecting Irish poetry top table publishing such a poem. And the idea that such a poem would ever be allowed pour its glorious contempt from the main stage at any of our posher literary festivals is laughable. In the crisis years since 2008,

[8] Fictional townland in UK television crime drama

literary festivals have, among other things, become places Irish Times readers go to be reassured that, despite Trump, despite Brexit, despite the yobbos of the anti-water charges movement, everything is going to be alright. Such gatherings are increasingly the intellectual equivalent of a pampering spa with a seaweed bath, places people with above average incomes – and sometimes sons and daughters of theirs who aspire to be writers - go to retreat from ugly realities and remind themselves how progressive they are.

There are recent poems which resist this trend. 'The People Died', from Dublin poet Karl Parkinson's most recent book, *Sacred Symphonies* is a most blatant example:: "They died eating Coco Pops, and starting the day with an Actimel/...They died while tweeting lies about immigrants and queers/...They died jerking off to Tik Tok in their one bedroom council flat/...They died of cervical cancer they were told they did not have..." And then Parkinson takes fabulous aim at the current occupants of the best room: "You are the murderers of poetry: / your lines wait like creeps in alleyways, /... your stanzas so boring they make a glory of ironing..." It is those later lines that will most likely debar Parkinson from the room, though he is, in truth, generous in his judgement, for the typical literary networker is in all likelihood far more mercenary than the average creep in an alleyway. Working class poets will be allowed in, as long as they ditch barbed critiques of the Parkinson/Eluard variety, acquire an agent, and join what I call the My Old Man's A Dustman school. The government funded bouncers who guard poetry's best room quite enjoy non-threatening verse anecdotes about life among the lower orders, especially when told in a suitably charming inner-city accent.

Other poems, such as Jane Clarke's 'Who Owns The Field', from her debut collection *The River* (Bloodaxe, 2015) and Ruth Quinlan's 'The Corrib Great Southern Hotel' which appeared in the most recent edition of *The Stinging Fly* challenge the assumptions of the occupants of Irish poetry's best room, particularly those who consider themselves to be in favour of equality, and are, as long as that equality remains entirely abstract and doesn't get in the way of their quiet worship of those who own things. Clarke's poem is influenced by Kavanagh, for sure. But, to me, the question it politely, but directly, asks has as much in common with the radical realism of 19th century French painters such as Millet:

Who Owns The Field

Is it the one who is named in the deeds
whose hands never touched the clay
or is the one who gathers the sheaves,

takes a scythe to the thistles, plants the beech,
digs out the dockweed, lays the live hazel?

Most of those who dwell permanently in Irish literature's best room will listen to this poem, while sipping sugary tea from a fine cup, and pretend they side, obviously, it goes without saying, with the one who "takes a scythe to the thistles". In reality, if someone like this turned up at a poetry reading, their skin would crawl just a little. Even if he had the manners to leave his scythe at home. And if someone with such an obvious lack of bourgeois refinement were given a spot at a poetry open-mic to read one of his own poems, they would discover they urgently had to leave. As they swept out the door, probably sporting some sort of cloak with a Celtic design on it, they'd make a mental note to remind themselves to suggest at the next meeting of the arts organisation board they are a member of that "the one who is named in the deeds", mentioned at the start of Jane Clarke's poem, be invited onto said board as a representative of the "business community". Quinlan's 'The Corrib Great Southern, 2020' takes a look at the catastrophe sometimes imposed upon communities by "the one who is named in the deeds". The Corrib Great Southern was a huge, successful hotel on the eastern outskirts of Galway City. It was originally one of a chain of state owned hotels. As well as being a hotel, its bar and restaurant were much used by people on Galway's east side, which is not very well served in such matters. Then it was sold off because that was the Progressive Democrat[9] thing to do. In 2007 it ceased to be a functioning hotel

---

[9] Irish political party, now defunct, on the ultra end of the neo-liberal spectrum

because the dashing local entrepreneur who bought it had better ideas. But then 2008 came and said entrepreneur was much in need of government help, which he got. But the Corrib Great Southern, which you can't miss as you enter Galway via the Dublin Road, was left to rot. It is now to be demolished but its demolition has been delayed due to Covid. During its almost decade and a half of dereliction, it has been stripped of everything of value, and become a favourite haunt of arsonists:

The scavengers come, Egyptian plovers
that pluck debris from between the teeth
of this bloated, stranded reptile,

this grounded giant that bequeathed its wings
as verdigris sails to the building next door.
It has surrendered to waiting for death

by a hundred attempts at arson,
until the inferno that cracks its bones
back down to the rebar marrow.

Quinlan's poem is an Irish 'Ozymandias'. But unlike Shelley's Ozymandias, whose power was so distant as to be beyond memory – the Pharaoh's monument to himself sinking into the sand vainly shouting: "My name is Ozymandias, King of Kings; / Look on my Works, ye Mighty, and despair!" – the developer genius who shut the Corrib Great Southern down in 2007 still stalks the business community like so many other zombies and has lately been chosen as the "preferred bidder" for Galway's proposed new "Ceannt Quarter" on land currently owned by CIE[10]. This development may, apparently, include some "arts space". Ruth Quinlan's poem works in the negative, it doesn't envisage alternatives, but it takes the first crucial step by graphically imagining this giant local symbol of the existing Fine Fail/Fianna Gael order going up in flames its owners brought upon it.

Most of the poems that have emerged from Irish poetry's best room over the past decade imagine no such flames. It is a failure of the imagination, a sign in some cases of terminal decadence, that after more than a decade of economic and social crisis most 'serious' contemporary Irish poetry appears unable to imagine any possibility other than the ongoing rule of people like the aforementioned "preferred bidder". For the most part, the question seems not to even cross its mind. The only explanation for this is a Marxist one: the literary wing of Ireland's establishment, deep down in its faintly pumping heart, agrees that there is, in the words of the late Margaret Thatcher, no alternative. Yes, there will be occasional bleating about the need for better ethics legislation and the like. And poems about the undeniable sins and abuses of the Ireland of yesterdecade are available by the truckload. But when it comes to our actual present day rulers, people like the guy who made the Corrib Great Southern a place fit only for rats and arsonists, a hush falls over most of the

[10] Irish government owned public transport company

distinguished occupants of Irish poetry's best and, if truth were told, silliest room. The result is a lot of well written poems which mostly seem to me to be beside the point. Contemporary Irish poetry is very brave when it comes to kicking long dead Archbishops.

Of course there is more than one way to get the occupants of the best room not-very-quietly grinding their teeth. While Karl Parkinson does so by reminding the assembled casual jackets and trousers suits just how conservative they really are, poets such as Rachel Coventry and Patrick Chapman do so primarily by appearing to reject the alleged interestingness – held sacrosanct in some of the best room's better quality armchairs – of the lives and attitudes of the liberal humanists who infest academia, the arts, and 'quality' media, for whom having once been against Apartheid, or being for ending Direct Provision[11], or Repealing The 8th Amendment, were/are less about overturning bourgeois society than about hopefully getting themselves invited on the Marian Finucane Show[12] (RIP) and perhaps eventually being appointed as a member of the Arts Council by some 'progressive' future Minister, probably on the same day the government finally decides to cut the pretence and abolish corporation tax altogether, and to incentivise investment further by offering visiting Facebook executives complimentary use of high end sex workers dressed in Irish dancing costumes.

The North London squatters, heroin users, and lifestyle anarchists who largely populate Rachel Coventry's

[11] Irish government detention system for asylum seekers

[12] Irish television and radio broadcaster

debut *Afternoon Drinking In The Jolly Butchers* (Salmon, 2018) share one thing in common with the people in Karl Parkinson's poems: if they came anywhere near one of Irish poetry's quality armchairs, the Gardaí would be called. Coventry doesn't romanticise - her portraits do not eschew brutality - but neither does she condemn by implying, as others would, that all the characters in her poems need to do to solve their lives is move to Tudor Lawn, and spend their evenings googling the cheapest possible car insurance. In her first collection at least, Coventry is closer to Baudelaire than she is to the aforementioned quality armchairs, the title poem brings to brilliant life the world of people most polite society considers "wasters", and what's more shows some of those wasters to be at least as intelligent as your average car insurance googler:

They tell me now
each decision
opens a rift between
this world and
a possible one.
Even trivial stuff
a tea or a latte
splits us endlessly
so now you and me
as we turned out
are galaxies apart
from the last time we agreed
the last time you asked me

shall we have another one?

In the late eighties and early nineties I lived a few miles up the road from Coventry, though I didn't know her then, and participated in such discussions, though in those days my answer was always a political one because back then I knew everything. I can see the jukebox in that pub, I can taste the chicken and chips we'd get on the way back to someone's gaff as our great debate continued. This poem made me miss the people I knew back there; and this is a rare thing, for such people hardly ever turn up in contemporary Irish poems, to which such hardened 'wasters' are, generally speaking, not admitted.

Ever since the publication of his early collections almost thirty years ago, Patrick Chapman has been quietly working to ensure his more or less permanent exclusion from the best room. An early collection was titled *The New Pornography* (Salmon, 1996). Clear evidence that Chapman, despite his gentle, unthreatening manner was a likely bringer of unseemliness rather than a potential poet-priest of the sort Official Irish Poetry is always on the lookout for. In a short poem from that collection Chapman disturbs the peace of post-Cold War liberal euphoria by writing in 'The Communist':

I am buying dead atlases – drawn up
Before a port wine stain became our map –
To stack them, thousands tall,
Like bricks in some new Berlin Wall.

Back then, in their super-confident high summer of the 1990s, the liberal humanists could safely chuckle at such a piece of literary mischief. Now, given the considerable nostalgia for Stalinism in Russia, parts of Eastern Europe, and indeed elsewhere, the liberal humanist is less likely to chuckle than s/he is to start spluttering conspiracy theories about how Hilary was robbed by Putin and Putin's evil side kick: Julian Assange. Chapman, though, is, like Coventry, more in the school of Baudelaire (with bit of JG Ballard thrown in to bring things up to date) than he is in the school of Brecht/Swift. His 2007 collection *Breaking Hearts and Traffic Lights* (Salmon) is entirely made up of love poems, each of them written to a different person, and one of them titled 'Mercy Fuck'. Chapman's most recent collection *Open Season On The Moon* (Salmon, 2019) includes 'Zen Strangler':

to kill is an act
of three perfect moves it takes
rare precision to

execute in one
instant the trained assassin
must break the windpipe

there is no second
attempt either the target
is ended or not

a killing has no
tenses no rhyme no season
the master moves like

lightening strike be gone
he cannot make a proper
kill if he's not

always prepared he
sits in his Zen rockery
all day everyday

meditating on
the moment his hands are so
attuned to even

the slightest flutter
of a cherry petal...

The poem's mockery of the Zen pretentions of many wealthy European and North American post-Christians is emphasised by the fact the poem is written as a series of Haiku (or near Haiku). After reading it, I closed my eyes and visualised Elon Musk reciting Chapman's poem, while rattling a tiny tambourine, during his 4am daily meditation. Poetry's best room is littered with ageing post-Christians who have a great fondness for eastern promise of the sort disturbingly, and brilliantly, lampooned by Chapman. He shouldn't expect to be invited into the sanctum any time soon.

Dave Lordan is a rarity in Irish poetry, an open revolutionary socialist who is also a poet of sublime skills. His work combines the beautiful brutality of the Brecht/Swift school with the couldn't-give-a-shit shrug of the Baudelaire school. Lordan's first collection *The Boy In The Ring* (Salmon, 2007) won both the Patrick Kavanagh Award and the Strong Award for Best first collection. In 2012, after the publication of his second book *Invitation to a Sacrifice* (Salmon, 2010), Lordan was awarded The Chair of Ireland Poetry Bursary. The title poem from his 2014 collection *Lost Tribe of The Wicklow Mountains* (Salmon, 2014) provided the lyrics for a song which featured on Christy Moore's 2016 album *Lily*. Having won every award available to a new Irish poet, and also achieved a readership (and listenership) that stretched well beyond the usual, Lordan appeared to be on his way to being allowed rest his glutes in one of those fine armchairs.

Lordan's initial mainstream success was a way literary Ireland could demonstrate the enormity of its own tolerance. But as the political situation here became more unstable with the emergence of the anti-water privatisation movement in 2014-16 – a movement which as well as defeating water charges also put an at least temporary stop to austerity – the tolerance of the arts libs was at an end. The alternative literature blog, *The Bogman's Cannon,* which Lordan co-edited with Karl Parkinon throughout 2015 and 2016, relished in the (to us) thrilling new political situation. This provoked the raw hatred of many government funded arts liberals, and a few of those who aspire to be government funded. These people are, of course, all for equality as long as equality is something to be parcelled out to those in need of it by committees of people like themselves. But the anti-water charges movement was viewed by most arts libs as being a rather aggressive movement of smelly people which, like Republicanism in the North, needed to be put back in its box so that civilisation could continue. The way Lordan combined activist socialism of the non Ivana Bacik variety with the business of being a poet, made it essential he be ejected. It is a loss because it now means that the official list of best Irish poets now writing is basically a lie. But then such lists often are a lie. And Lordan's exclusion from it puts him in esteemed company. The brilliantly innovative Scottish poet, Tom Leonard, author of the hilarious satire on the BBC 'The Six O'Clock News' (1970) was similarly not invited to sit at the top table for many years, before his death in 2018, for reasons that appear to be entirely political. American poet Muriel Rukeyser (1913-1980), whose gloriously dismissive poem 'More of A Corpse Than A Woman' I often use in workshops, was a leading young poet of the 1930s but fell dramatically out of favour during the political witch-hunts of the late 40s and early 1950s because of her communist sympathies. Closer to home, Thomas Kinsella suddenly became much less famous after the publication in 1972 of his poem 'Butcher's Dozen', an unceremoniously Swiftian attack on the Widgery

Tribunal's[13] obvious cover up of the massacre by the British Army of civil rights protestors in Derry. A giant historical example of such politically motivated marginalisation of a poet was that inflicted on John Milton after the restoration of the monarchy in 1660. Milton was jailed for a time and in serious fear of his life, given his role as Cromwell's Latin Secretary during the Commonwealth, in which capacity he wrote the legal justification for the execution of Charles I. His great epic 'Paradise Lost', itself an allegory for the failure of his faction to turn England into a Republic, was published in an almost underground fashion in 1667. And the monarchists still haven't forgiven Milton; as recently as 1936 that well known bestower of kisses on royal and high Anglican bottoms, T.S. Eliot, was arguing that Milton was a "bad influence" on the poets of subsequent centuries. Eliot pretended that his hostility to Milton was politically disinterested. Just like the high priests and priestesses of the (entirely government funded) best room today like to let on that their non-election of Lordan is a matter devoid of politics. It is in the company of such giants that Lordan's poetry must eventually take its place. But for now the poetry quangocrats still wield their bit of power, like latter day Zhdanov's[14] , only with far inferior politics and without those superb buttoned jackets. Though there is dissent from the prevailing wish of most of the occupants of the best room that Lordan, and his poetry, should just

---

[13] 1972 British government investigation into Bloody Sunday massacre by British Army. Its finding are now discredited.

[14] Soviet cultural ideologist under Josef Stalin

cease to exist. Áosdána member and almost universally respected poet Thomas McCarthy recently had this to say:

> *I feel ashamed that he [Lordan] is not more widely celebrated. He really deserves to be. His is a very new voice, developing a new method, less attached to Auld Decencies and old venerable names in poetry but more attached to the pulsing, angry, precise moment; sometimes emotionally overwhelmed by the very choice of hard material, but overwhelmed in the best way as he's dealing with new sensibilities in an exiled Joycean way; and new, detached, bleak insights into the sheer cruelty of Irish life and how this life has betrayed a generation – a generation of demotic provincials as well as the educated travelled young of the cities.*

Another poet who has equivalent skills and similar politics to Lordan, though a somewhat milder poetic persona, is Ciarán O'Rourke, whose debut *The Buried Breath* was published by Irish Pages in 2018. O'Rourke is a more controlled, less brash, poet than Lordan. For me, the tone of some of his work calls to mind the surgical accuracy of great Eastern European poets such as Zbigniew Herbert or, at times, the fabulist lyricism of Neruda, rather than the louchness of Baudelaire or the brazen attempt to appeal to a wide non-literary public of writers of the Brecht/Swift school. O'Rourke is a profoundly literary poet. *The Buried Breath* includes translations of Virgil and Catullus and "variations"on poems by Rubén Darío, Antonio Machada, and Roque Dalton. On evidence of his poem 'The

Revolutionist', if the Fine Gael[15] wing of poetry's best room, those now permanently attached to its grandest chairs, ever get to organise McCarthy style 'investigations' into poets suspected of being secretly okay with Ireland's corporate tax rate being increased to 13%, O'Rourke can expect a subpoena:

And so I say the earth
is beautiful,

and belongs
like poetry or bread

to all of us,
who despite love's

poisoned battleground
are believers still

in the pungent roots
that smell like tears,

in the streaming grain
or tomorrow's skies,

in the billowing verb
of the blood we share –

---

[15] Right of centre Irish political party. In government at time of writing.

we who have faced
the hungry future singing,

the earth belongs to all of us,
like poetry, like bread.

There is a revolutionary call to, if not arms, then certainly action implicit in O'Rourke's poem. This will not go down well among the shakers and movers in the room. And it's not that they think revolution is impractical or utopian; it's that the bulk of them don't want to even begin imagining a time when "the earth belongs to all of us, / like poetry, like bread" because they think the earth, and poetry, should belong to people like them. The word "us" is used by the average poetry networker far less often than the word "me". It would be wrong to say that such people have no politics at all, they do; mostly still subscribing to the pre-2008 mirage that, if only Ireland could have a few more tribunals of investigation into political corruption and past abuses by the church, then it might, as the IRA and the Catholic Church vanish, become something called a Modern European Democracy, which mostly seems to mean some imaginary version of Belgium or Denmark which exist only in the heads of Irish liberal humanists. This imaginary Modern European Democracy would continue to be a loyal colony of the European Union, loyally nodding its agreement to things like the starving of Greece into submission in 2015 and would be prepared to allow a few more of its citizens to die of Covid (possibly including me[16]) rather than go outside the EU structure and buy the Russian Sputnik vaccine. The Modern Democratic Ireland they imagine would also continue to gratefully present the annual bowl of shamrock to whatever corporate shill or assorted maniac inhabits the White House that St. Patrick's Day. Most crucial of all its corporate tax rate would remain - for all eternity world-without-end Amen - 12.5%, and a lot less for Google.

The work of contemporary Irish poets such as Parkinson, Quinlan, Coventry, Chapman, Lordan, and O'Rourke has helped me stay, to some extent, sane as I have moved ever further away from poetry's best room over the past decade. Revolutionary songs such as Dominic Behan's 'McAlpine's Fuseliers' and Moving Hearts' 'No Time For Love' have also been a sustaining resource. For me, they are two of the best Irish political poems since the Second World War. Similarly, working with my poetry workshop groups has been a great source of sanity retention. Whatever their subject, there is something inherently liberating, revolutionary even, about the first few breakthrough poems a poet writes. Though that revolution will slowly be overthrown if, having become aware of its existence, the poet decides they must do what needs to be done, say what needs to be said, to get into the best room. I have also found valuable allies among the dead, who have one huge advantage: they never argue

---

[16] See this article https://www.irishtimes.com/life-and-style/health-family/dreams-in-which-only-the-monsters-are-real-1.4240988

back. Particularly crucial in this regard have been the examples of my personal hero Swift, Bertolt Brecht, and on my zanier, more disgraceful, days, Andre Breton and Baudelaire.

During that time some first rate new Irish poets have established themselves and been given their due recognition. A standout is Ailbhe Darcy who in her T.S. Eliot Award nominated second collection *Insistence* (Bloodaxe, 2018) – particularly in her formally audacious twenty page poem 'Alphabet' – is prepared to at least countenance the entirely plausible notion that we just might all be doomed:

We are not doomed yet

juggle the numbers

some of us are doomed
but not the 3 of us

or not the three of us
just yet

or maybe 1 of us,
the smallest,

the 1 of us
still learning
numbers,

who doesn't know
what 2 of us
are keeping to ourselves...

The spiky wit that is Martina Evans has, since the publication of her *The Windows of Graceland: New & Selected Poems* (Carcanet, 2016), begun to get something like proper acknowledgment. She writes brilliantly about things like having a tooth rather brutally pulled and lowers the tone in a way of which I entirely approve by giving her poems titles such as 'Fine Gael Form a Coalition Government with Labour, March 1973'. In many ways Evans is the poet Paul Durcan could still be, if he hadn't spent since around 1989 slowly becoming a poetic teddy bear for Conor Cruise O'Brien[17] fans who can't decide between voting Green and converting to Anglicanism, and are hoping Fintan O'Toole will give them some spiritual guidance on the matter.

Elsewhere, new reputations are inflated by the incessant behind the scenes puffing of the best room's Lord and Lady Archbishops. In the words of Alexander Pope: "Slight is the subject, but not so the praise". The new poets go up like helium balloons only to wait to be replaced by the next helium balloon who'll be along soon. And this is by no means an exclusively Irish phenomenon. In January, liberal humanists worldwide were brought to a state of simultaneous almost orgasm by the poem Amanda Gorman recited at the Biden inauguration. The New Yorker

[17] Former Irish Labour government minister who developed increasingly extreme anti-republican positions in relation to Northern Ireland

called Gorman's poem "a stunning vision of democracy". Jane Hirschfield got altogether more carried away, saying:

"The Hill We Climb felt to me just the perfect answer for this moment, its needs and its questions...New politics need new persons, and new poets...Amanda Gorman has invented something new here and in earlier poems, a kind of hybrid form: half poem, half spoken essay (a word that means, first, "to try" and has to do with thinking your way forward sentence by sentence). Her writing sits at a cloverleaf intersection, moving between lyric intensity and interiority, spoken-word and hip hop's combination of fluid rhyming and fierce examination of the world around us, and carrying the benevolence, eloquence, and hope-offering that can come from both podium and pulpit (at their best)."

Well, indeed. Objectively, 'The Hill We Climb' is a rhythmical collection of warmed over Obamaesque platitudes; devoid, so far as I could see, of one single original metaphor or simile: "we lift our gazes not to what stands between us, but what stands before us. / We close the divide because we know, to put our future first, we must first / put our differences aside". It goes on. But you get the idea. The politics underpinning it are also banal in that it seems to imply, and more than imply, that all America now needs do is return is to business as usual as it was between 2008-16, when Barack Obama presided over the largest ever transfer of wealth upwards from the pockets of the 99% into the bank accounts of the 1%. In an interview with George Stephanopoulos[18] in 2013, Obama himself agreed that "95% of income gains from 2009 to 2012 went to the top 1% of the earning population". But none of this matters because Gorman now has a modelling contract and has been interviewed for *Time* magazine by Michelle Obama.

In the past, the saving grace the occupants of poetry's best room could claim for themselves was that they and they alone were a kind of insurance against bad political poetry which was all and only about being on message. No more. The inauguration poem was every bit as bland as the poetry promoted by Commissar Zhdanov in his heyday and, if truth were told, probably a little worse. But from the best room it provoked mostly liberal humanist cheers or, in a few cases, silence, because, to paraphrase the character CJ from the *Fall and Rise of Reginald Perrin*[19], they didn't get where they are by publicly contradicting Jane Hirshfield.

Stranded in this strange world, what then is one to do? Keep going in the opposite direction. In the autumn of 2014 I received a Facebook message from Rhona McCord, who then worked for one of the left wing TDs in Leinster House. She jokily asked me where my poem about the exploding anti-water charges movement was? I started writing and the result was 'Irish Air: Message From The CEO', a modest proposal in which an apparently insane government spokesperson outlined plans to start charging people for air. The poem was shared on his Facebook page

[18] Former advisor to Bill Clinton. Now a television journalist.

[19] 1970s British television comedy series

by MEP Luke 'Ming' Flanagan[20] on the morning of one of the huge anti-water charges demos and went almost viral. It later appeared in my New & Selected Poems. In 2015, the day after Ed Miliband's defeat by David Cameron in the UK general election a visiting friend read from his phone that Tony Blair had an article in that Sunday's Observer newspaper arguing that UK Labour need to move back to the centre ground i.e. to be more for colonial wars and protecting the interests of the haves and the have mores than they already were. I said that I would rather make love to John Prescott[21], a large man who is not my type, than read Blair's article. Then I posted a comment to that effect on Twitter. Danny Morrison, the former Sinn Féin publicity director and spokesman for Bobby Sands during his hunger strike, replied that me declaring my preference for being taken by Lord Prescott, if the alternative was reading what Tony Blair had written, belonged in a poem. I subsequently wrote 'Blair's Advice', a poem which spoke in the voice of the sort of deranged pro things-as-they-were-in-1997 centrist who has been a permanent fixture on the political scene of late. The poem was published on The Bogman's Cannon, where I was satirist-in-residence at the time. It also appeared on the UK based site Socialist Unity. Within a few days The Morning Star newspaper got in touch to ask if they could also publish it. And then when it appeared there, the Irish Times asked if they could run the poem, and a short piece

[20] Member of Irish parliament (Dáil) 2011-16. Member of European Parliament since 2014.

[21] UK Deputy Prime Minister 1997-2007

about it, on their online pages. In accepting Rhona McCord and Danny Morrison's suggestions/challenges to write the poems that became 'Irish Air: Message From The CEO' & 'Blair's Advice' I was doing the opposite of what Seamus Heaney once famously did. It was with Danny Morrison that Heaney had the exchange on a train during the dirty protests, which preceded the 1980 and 1981 hunger strikes, that is infamously poeticised in Heaney's poem 'Flight Path':

So he enters and sits down
Opposite and goes for me head on.
'When, for fuck's sake, are you going to write
Something for us?' 'If I do write something,
Whatever it is, I'll be writing for myself.'
And that was that. Or words to that effect.

In the book of interviews with Heaney, *Stepping Stones* by Dennis O'Driscoll, published in 2009, Heaney admits: "I make the speaker a bit more aggressive than he was at the time." Such exaggerations are what poets do. All of us. For us that is not a sin. Though our victims may not always see it that way. In a 2006 interview with Gavin Esler on the BBC to mark the 40th anniversary of the publication of his debut collection *Death of A Naturalist*, Heaney had this to say about his tendency to resist giving support to any given political cause: "Once a writer is levied or enlisted you have lost your self respect, which is a writer's only passport to the future". There are different ways in which a poet can be enlisted, though. Almost every major English speaking political corpse this side of Henry Kissinger and Mother Teresa has chosen to publicly quote Heaney's "hope and history" line. That is not his fault. But it is proof that, despite wishing to maintain one's political neutrality, one can be enlisted nevertheless. Not writing poems "for us" can lead to a poet being co-opted by them.

Since 2014, I have written many poems which are "for us" rather than for them. But I am not worried about becoming a party hack. A good section of the left is at least suspicious of me, for the shots I took at them in poems between 2008 and 2014. But when I write what Dave Lordan has called "interventionist poems" I don't write poems to support particular little political factions. I write them to support, and just as importantly to record, the progressive movements of our time. The Repeal the 8th Amendment movement, the Ant-Water Charges movement, the Corbyn movement, the Bernie movement, Black Lives Matter, the radical end of the Extinction Rebellion movement, and whatever comes next.

The occupants of Irish poetry's best room are most of them pretty clearly enlisted in the broadly centrist faction who'd like things to calm down and to see some decorum restored to our public discourse so that Eamon Ryan and Joan Burton no longer get laughed at on Twitter. I have no such desire for calmness or decorum. Indeed, my satirical poems aim to make the laughter louder and, hopefully, a little more stylish. I still write many poems which are not at all overtly political. But many of them are far too disgraceful to be considered applications to be let into the best room.

I am happy where I am. The last few years have been politically thrilling times. And the chance to respond to them in poems has been a dark joy. Covid times have been particularly tough for me, though. One of my favourite things in the world is poetry world gossip. It's one of the things I have most missed. And it's just not the same online. I look forward to the next few years when I fully expect most of the little liberal poets, every one of them desperate for an invitation to read one of their poems to the President of somewhere, to slowly turn into the late Marion Finucane, still kicking the occasional dead Archbishop every so often as they go, just to prove how edgy they are. Respected pillars of things as they absolutely must be (above all our unmentionably holy 12.5% corporate tax rate). Or, if they are too male for their atrophy to take that particular physical form, they'll likely become versions of the guy who entered Neachtains Bar in Galway about thirty five years ago sporting a big 'left wing' beard with a good dose of grey in it. Teenage me was there with a slightly older friend who turned and whispered: "that guy probably thinks he's a Trotskyist but also thinks that, right now, the best we can hope for is Garret Fitzgerald[22]." The

---

[22] Irish Prime Minister (Taoiseach) for much of 1980s who presided over mass unemployment, austerity, the return of emigration, and attempted liberal social reforms

next few years are, in the words of Miranda's[23] mother, going to be "such fun!" I can't wait.

[23] Main character in eponymous UK television comedy farce 2009 onwards

ACKNOWLEDGEMENTS: acknowledgements are due to the following publications in which this essay, or extracts from it, first appeared: *Village Magazine, The Morning Star, Rochford Street Review, Cassandra Voices, Vox Galvia – The Galway Advertiser, & Contemporary Irish Literature Research Network.*
Cover image - Higgins chairing a political public meeting about South Africa the day before his 17th birthday taken by John Cunningham.

About the author

Kevin Higgins is co-organiser of Over The Edge literary events in Galway. He has published five full collections of poems: *The Boy With No Face* (2005), *Time Gentlemen, Please* (2008), *Frightening New Furniture* (2010), *The Ghost In The Lobby* (2014), & Sex *and Death at Merlin Park Hospital* (2019). His poems also feature in *Identity Parade – New British and Irish Poets* (Bloodaxe, 2010) and in *The Hundred Years' War: modern war* poems (Ed Neil Astley, Bloodaxe May 2014). Kevin was satirist-in-residence with the alternative literature website The Bogman's Cannon 2015-16. *2016 – The Selected Satires of Kevin Higgins* was published by NuaScéalta in 2016. *The Minister For Poetry Has Decreed* was published by Culture Matters (UK) also in 2016. *Song of Songs 2:0 – New & Selected Poems* was published by Salmon in Spring 2017. Kevin is a highly experienced workshop facilitator and several of his students have gone on to achieve publication success. He has facilitated poetry workshops at Galway Arts Centre and taught Creative Writing at Galway Technical Institute for the past fifteen years. Kevin is the Creative Writing Director for the NUI Galway International Summer School and also teaches on the NUIG BA Creative Writing Connect programme.

About the author

His poems have been praised by, among others, Tony Blair's biographer John Rentoul, Observer columnist Nick Cohen, writer and activist Eamonn McCann, historian Ruth Dudley Edwards, and Sunday Independent columnist Gene Kerrigan; and have been quoted in *The Daily Telegraph, The Independent, The Times* (London), *Hot Press* magazine, *The Daily Mirror* and on *The Vincent Browne Show,* and read aloud by Ken Loach at a political meeting in London. He has published topical political poems in publications as various as *The New European, The Morning Star, Dissent Magazine* (USA), *Village Magazine* (Ireland), & *Harry's Place. The Stinging Fly* magazine has described Kevin as "likely the most widely read living poet in Ireland". One of Kevin's poems features in *A Galway Epiphany,* the final instalment of Ken Bruen's Jack Taylor series of novels which is just published. His work has been broadcast on RTE Radio, Lyric FM, and BBC Radio 4. His book *The Colour Yellow & The Number 19: Negative Thoughts That Helped One Man Mostly Retain His Sanity During 2020* is just published by Nuascealta. Kevin's sixth full poetry collection, *Ecstatic,* will be published by Salmon in March 2022. **Website:** http://mentioningthewar.blogspot.com/ **Twitter:** @KevinHIpoet1967

Words of Praise

"I would never accuse Kevin Higgins of writing anything so diminishing as a rallying cry or manifesto. And yet, nobody is safe from his sharpened wit (least of all his Granny's fading crockery) as he eviscerates any notions we might have about what poetry should be. It would be wise to read this with a strong dose of self-awareness and, at the very least, a muted understanding of the genuine need for change in a world cracking under the weight of capitalism."

- **Alvy Carragher,** poet & author of *The Men I Keep Under My Bed* (Salmon Poetry, 2021)

Words of Praise

"Those who habitually occupy 'the best room' will hear its walls rattling in this detailed, rollicking, humorous, full-on piece of polemic. It's personal. What makes it even more forceful is that Higgins comes to praise as well as to bury, generously listing and quoting from a phalanx of poets. Poets who, while sometimes outside 'the best room', are making the best noises. In an age where poets are being routinely enlisted to make banks and building societies look 'street' [and themselves vacuous] ----this type of corrective slap is ever more necessary. Long may he [purposefully] rave."

- **Matthew Caley**, poet & author of Trawlerman's Turquoise (Bloodaxe Books, 2019)

Beir Bua

Press

www.BeirBuaPress.com

ISBN: 978-1-914972-07-2

9 781914 972072

Lightning Source UK Ltd.
Milton Keynes UK
UKHW022052201221
395986UK00011B/2853

9 781914 972072